You and Me

You and Me
ABC

Jennifer Blizin Gillis

Heinemann Library
Chicago, Illinois

Designed by Sue Emerson, Heinemann Library; Page layout by Que-Net Media™
Printed and bound in China by South China Printing Company Limited
Photo research by Janet Lankford Moran

08 07 06 05 04
10 9 8 7 6 5 4 3 2 1

Library of Congress Cataloging-in-Publication Data
Gillis, Jennifer
    You and me ABC / Jennifer Gillis.
        p. cm. – (You and me)
Summary: The letters of the alphabet are used to introduce examples of good behavior.
    ISBN 1-4034-2510-8 (HC), 1-4034-2512-4 (Pbk.)
    1. Etiquette for children and teenagers. 2. English language–Alphabet–Juvenile literature. [1. Conduct of life.
2. Alphabet.] I. Title.
    BJ1857.C5J597 2003
    395.1'22–dc22

JJR
395
GIL

2003012850

Acknowledgments
The author and publishers are grateful to the following for permission to reproduce copyright material:
p. 3 Getty Images; p. 4 Robert Lifson/Heinemann Library; p. 5 Ariel Skelley/Corbis; p. 6 Doug Mazell/Indexstock; pp. 7, 18 Myrleen Ferguson Cate/PhotoEdit Inc.; pp. 8, 15 Richard Hutchings/PhotoEdit Inc.; p. 9 Laura Dwight/Corbis; p. 10 ; p. 11 Warling Studios/Heinemann Library; pp. 12, 13 Que-Net/Heinemann Library; p. 14 Mary Kate Denny/PhotoEdit Inc.; p. 16 Bonnie Kamin/PhotoEdit Inc.; p. 17 Janet L. Moran/Oijoy Photography; p. 19 Ronnie Kaufman/Corbis; p. 20 Photodisc/Getty Images; p. 21 Jose Luis Pelaez, Inc./Corbis; p. 22 Norbert Schaefer/Corbis; p. 23 (T-B) Ariel Skelley/Corbis, Getty Images, Robert Lifson/Heinemann Library; p. 24 (T-B) Getty Images, Robert Lifson/Heinemann Library, Ariel Skelley/Corbis; back cover (L-R) Warling Studios/Heinemann Library, Que-Net/Heinemann Library

Cover photographs by (top left) Doug Mazell/Indexstock, (top right) Getty Images; (bottom center) Laura Dwight/Corbis

BtT 9/2004 $10.00

Every effort has been made to contact copyright holders of any material reproduced in this book. Any omissions will be rectified in subsequent printings if notice is given to the publisher.

Special thanks to our advisory panel for their help in the preparation of this book:
Alice Bethke, Library Consultant
Palo Alto, CA

Eileen Day, Preschool Teacher
Chicago, IL

Kathleen Gilbert,
Second Grade Teacher
Round Rock, TX

Sandra Gilbert,
Library Media Specialist
Fiest Elementary School
Houston, TX

Jan Gobeille,
Kindergarten Teacher
Garfield Elementary
Oakland, CA

Angela Leeper,
Educational Consultant
Wake Forest, NC

A a Able
B b Busy

We are able to do things for others.

We are never too busy to help out.

C c Care
D d Difference

We care about our neighborhood.

We can make a difference in the world around us.

E e Everyone
F f Fairness

We can be kind to everyone.

Everyone should be treated with fairness.

G g Good citizen

We try to be good citizens.

Good citizens care about
their community.

H h Help

We help at home and at school.

Work gets done faster when people help each other!

I i Individual

Each person is an individual.

This means that everyone is different in a special way.

J j Judge

We try not to judge other people.

This is another way of saying we try to be fair to everyone.

K k Kindness

We can take time to show kindness.

Being kind to others makes us feel better.

L l Listen

We listen while someone else is talking.

When we listen, we can learn new things.

11

M m Meet
N n New friend

When we go places, we meet other people.

Sometimes, we meet a new friend.

O o Old friends

When we make a new friend, we still play with our old friends.

New friends and old friends are the best kinds of friends there are!

P p Peace

We try to be at peace
with everyone.

This means we talk things out
without fighting or hitting.

Q q Quiet

When someone else is talking we are quiet.

R r Respect
S s School

When we are polite to others, we are showing respect.

We always show respect to our teachers and classmates at school.

T t   Trust

We show people that they can trust us.

This means that we always try to make the right choices.

U u   Useful

When we help others we are being useful.

V v Visit

A visit from friends can help
someone feel happy.

W w Wait
X x Exciting

When we want to do something, we wait for our turn.

It can be hard to wait for something exciting!

Y y You

You are powerful.

You have the power to create many things.

Z z Zoom

After dinner, we don't just zoom off.

We help with the dishes.

Quiz

Can you put these words in ABC order?

Look for the answer on page 24.

 Everyone

Fairness

 Able

Busy

 Care

Difference

Note to Parents and Teachers

Using this book, children can practice alphabetic skills while learning about character. Together, read *You and Me ABC.* As you discuss the concepts, say the names of the letters of the alphabet out loud. Then say the target word, exaggerating the beginning of the word. For example, "/r/: Rrrrr-espect." Can the child think of other words that begin with the /r/ sound? (Although the letter x is not at the beginning of the word "exciting," the /ks/ sound of the letter x is still prominent.) Try to sing the "ABC Song," substituting the *You and Me* alphabet words for the letters a, b, c and so on.

Index

Answer to quiz on page 22

Able

Busy

Care

Difference

Everyone

Fairness